Happiest Moments of My Life

Pearl Rock

authorHOUSE®

AuthorHouse™
1663 Liberty Drive
Bloomington, IN 47403
www.authorhouse.com
Phone: 833-262-8899

Published by AuthorHouse 07/28/2023

ISBN: 979-8-8230-1254-6 (sc)
ISBN: 979-8-8230-1253-9 (e)

Library of Congress Control Number: 2023914257

Contents

Believe in yourself, attuned with nature and the universe.

If you are happy now, you will be happy forever.

My positivity and lucks went me through.

Before you read

I put my soul in this book.

What is different from other authors' books is it included my background and my original stories and my personality.

I am writing to you.

But those are my real thoughts I keep reminding myself of.

In this opportunity, I would like to share them with you.

I could not be the happiest person in the world, but I feel the happiest. You can be happy if your mindset is nurtured.

My life has not been always easy but each and every single moment, day, I can embrace them.

This moment could be pivotal in your life.

I like seeing myself walking on the street in a daily life.

This kind of regular moment is the most precious to me.

Always you should be centred in the now.

The biggest gift I have got is my positive personality.

My friend says never met someone who is so optimistic.

Nonetheless, it took some time to reach the moment.

I don't simply throw away the past.

They are my footsteps.

I clearly remember I was there.

Many books gave me great insights.

I talk about basically everything about life.

This might look disorganised, but this is the entity of me.

On writing this book

"Masters have got more adversity in life"

They are the master of mistakes as a result in whatever area they are in.

They may not be as conscious but they in fact experienced enough ugly past and grow into those great masters.

They lived first so they can teach you.

How they have overcome those tough moments is different to each master but

They sure overthought and figure them out and got the answers by themselves.

What this book can benefit you

I wrote this book revealing my insecurities in full transparency, so it is my original book written from both personal and objective perspective.

This is the book of my life lessons and the biggest advice I can provide, throughout my daily life.

All those I wrote are based on my mistakes.

What I advise you is also what I remind myself of constantly.

<u>What parts of this book can attract you?</u>
<u>What is the difference compared to other books?</u>

Every book even in a same genre is different.

Every book includes different stories and the person's background.

This is my biography.

I can only capture a life like this.

This book represents my life itself.

Notice

- This book is written in my perspective, so it is not an example.

  Please take it as one person's idea in the whole wide world.

- I could be extremely straightforward in order to make my points clear.

  I know life is hard.

  With that in mind, I wrote it as positively as possible.

- The contents might look disorganized, but that messiness is entity of my honest thoughts.

- There is also contradiction in my thoughts which I am fully aware of, as things are interconnected, and a single thing could cover all too.

- When I ask a question in a book, please have a think.

Chapter 1

Who I am

who I am

Part 1 My personality and the principles
Part 2 My upbringings to the reborn

Part I My personality

I am now in south-west England a naturally blessed peaceful and quiet town.

This environment in terms of the place, the people around me, the culture.

Those used to be what I aspired.

After getting independent, my personality and the privilege of my upbringings every more flourished.

Who am I?

My childhood fortune teller book once said that

"The gift of mine is the luck and positivity"

<u>My EXTREME personality</u>

1. Recklessness and sensitivity

   I overthink about what is unnecessary while I could be extremely bold about what I do sometimes.

2. 0 or 100%

   I cannot balance well but in a positive sense, I excel at focusing on the one.

3. seek newness

   I'd been thinking this quality was a bad thing, but it is rather natural as you are growing each moment.

4. too positive and very confident without reasons

   Now I gained a mix of ideology and reality

5. capable of appreciating the now

   It was not easy at first because I know what to do in my head but actions did not match but I could improve my behaviour by practice

My principle

1. Be optimistic, be happy, Enjoy the now!
2. Love yourself!
3. Never forget the application to the nature, to your support system, and anything you connect with!
4. Seek new inspiration!
5. Be hopeful and believe in yourself!
6. You focus on what you love to do!
7. Choose the difficult way and get out of your comfort zone!
8. Challenge yourself!
9. Believe in yourself!

Part 2 My upbringings to the reborn

Things I apricate my parents about

1. They let me experience whatever I wished to try generously.
2. They gave me potentials and confidence.
3. They give me bountiful love.

My role models

He is a perfect father of me, and a perfect husband of my mother.

He is passionate about his work.

He is a hard worker.

He is respectful.

He is generous. He gives.

He looks happy when his family is happy.

He does not complain about anything.

He works hard for the family.

He runs a business. He always has to keep his eyes of his conpany, which requires a large amount of will and self-control.

He just sleeps at home, coming back only for some hours sleep and next dawn he leaves home early.

That repeats throughout the year except for the weekends and the holidays when he looks for and get motivations from.

His aged t-shirt makes him greater.

He always wears the same colour and same design clothes, which modestly shows his discipline and devotion to his work.

He creates plenty of time for family time.

He is adventurous too. He likes to try new thing.

He teaches me by showing how to do

Greeting
He always suggested me to say "thank you" before you leave
a restaurant.

The spirit of the give
He often suggested me to give a seat to the next waiting family
in restaurant.

His lessons

THERE ARE THE UPS AND DOWNS IN LIFE.
IF THERE WAS A UP, THEN THERE
WILL BE A DOWN AND VICE VERSA.

BELIEVE WHAT YOU HAVE
CHOSEN IS THE BEST.

My confidence in childhood

Every story has a serious of scenes that are important to lead
the ending.

I was just a free-spirited and genuine girl.
I was the happiest child in the world.

I believe that my self-confidence came more naturally.

my family members always gave me positive comments on my personality and appearance.

I was even thinking that the world is revolving around me.

I think every child who was content with where they were might have felt this way. #

Because they are kids, so their imagination is a million of possibilities.

I was so luckily so I misinterpreted as a child.

Everything comes easy and everything is fun and happy for me, I guess.

I was the happiest child in the world.

I used to be very positive too.

<u>Is that from my parents' upbringing or the innate ability?</u>

I believe both are true.

the skill by nature helps boost up what I gain from the raising.

I was happy and positive. Always…

Additionally, I was confident about who I was.

Every parent of a child or a puppy tends to think they are the cutest and the best.

I was always in that bubble.

My mother said to me,

'You are the cutest in your grade!'

'You are the most beautiful girl in the band'

They lifted my confidence, but I would not necessarily compliment my child in that way that you compare your child with other kids.

'You are beautiful' this simple sentence sounds the best to me.

I did not know I had been so confident in myself and have been in a blessed environment.

I am happy now all thanks to them.

I felt very protective about my parents looking back.

I was writing letters and cry hard.

I dreamed often about rescuing my family.

I always put my family first which was always my TOP priority.

It partially comes from the Buddhism thoughts. The repay to parents.

Greeting, application, a repayment.

I was not this happy all the time, growing up, obviously.

Since I graduated from the elementary, I got more realistic.

Leave the past and the past-self in the past as your memory

The past.
What shaped you.
Your footsteps.
Something you can recall.
Something you should be proud of.
Something that should encourage you.

Even so, you should not hold on to the past long.

The past is the past.
You can tell your old stories.
But once it passed, it is in your past self.

What matters is what you can do now.

Each moment, you are evolving.
Each person is fighting on the same fair ground or should be.

The past does not necessarily define you.
Good or bad.

I don't like me sticking around the past and the past-self.
Not because they are negative.

But because you should appreciate the presence more.
For me I could not be happier in childhood.

My upbringing

I have no complains whatsoever, it was rather overwhelmingly supportive, warm,

loving.

My upbringing was utterly fortunate and plentiful with all my family members aligned, being there for me.

There was no divorce, I had two sets of grandparents, my family was close each other living in the same area

They never let me feel sad.

They took me any kinds of places, from the fancy places to natural places every weekend.

We travelled abroad in longer vocations.

They gave me great amount of potential and my family, and my experience made me confidence.

It multiplied.

Not having had those fortunate and caring childhood may have changed who I am now.

I am now even where I am

I imagine I would have been completely different.

I gained the success from happiness.

In that regard, I must not have had much trouble.

Until now

There are some pivotal moments in my life what shaped who I currently am.

I am changed, evolved as I got bigger.

But those memory never gets gone away forever. Where they are is in my drawer in my heart.

They are the greatest assets in my heart.

People say you get some very important milestone in your life.

Your carrier success, your marriage, your children.

I see the process getting those points. Those most amazing moments are unforgettable but very quick. You make endless effort to get those.

My high school

What are your memorable experience in high school?

For me, I don't come up with any popular events. The teachers told us that the school trips were going to be the most memorable. I got it that time, but I don't think so.

When I remember the most is just the everyday life. Particularly the last year in high school when I was conscious of what kind of person I am and each day with much application and sense of value.

The day after day.

I climb up the bridge in the morning in a hurry. It was always hard to get up there, peddling it at the standing position. And I see the stunning scenery. I know really how everyone feels that why on the bridge. I did every single time.

Friendships

<u>What is friendship?</u>

<u>I was always a loner.</u>
I was fully content with it, to cut straight to the point.
That was the best for me.

Some are on a completely different headspace.
I could not get along with those who speak discouraging comments often and those who are always unwilling to learn.

<u>Classroom could be like a prison.</u>
You cannot stay away unless classes finish.
I always wanted to get out there.
I did not speak but I express my thoughts on notebooks.

I am not sure if they are all my friends.
I had someone to hang out with at school or a group I was kind of in.

But they are not my true friends.

I could not open up and I could not be honest as I was certain that they won't get me.

Those are not worth opening myself up to.

I always believe that this is what I chose to be so I could be proud.

<u>The exceptional don't do well on the exams.</u>
I was always going the opposite ways from the ways teachers told me to do.

Because I knew it is not really beneficial for me.

The reborn

I always wanted to be independent, as I cannot rely on my parents' entitlement and privilege anymore.

So, I have moved on from the past at the early age.

I consider my family as my greatest responsibilities which I will give my favours back to.

I consider myself as an individual.

They are somebody I care and important.

I would like to think I don't belong to them anymore as I could count on them forever although I cannot.

<u>Then, I was reborn.</u>

The shift in time

What I dreamed all came to the reality. I embraced every moment. I even many times said to myself as loud as I could, I am now different with a new evolved self.

But they are all in the past.

Yesterday and tomorrow are two different things.

I feel the time passing by each moment.

What can you see NOW?
What are you thinking NOW?

What kind of person I want to be?

I would like to be a person who gives others a great sense of calmness when they are with me.

I would like to give my favours back to those who supported me in the past or when I was not being the best version of me.

Chapter 2

The Power of Each Moment

I don't belong to any religion, but I like the holistic concept for any religion.

DO WHAT YOU WANT THEM TO DO TO YOU.
DON'T DO WHAT YOU DON'T
WANT THEM TO DO TO YOU.

I am a believer in the now.

People read the Holy Bible because it helps stay where they should be.

Remember every breath and every step and every second is a change to renew yourself.

Never look back. Keep your favourite memory in the back of your drawer inside your heart.

The past and future are what you can recall and predict but

What matters is the now.

THE HAPPIER YOU ARE, THE MORE OPPORTUNITIES COME TO YOU.

I have been thinking about the past, the now and the future.

Who are you?

When you are out there with nothing.

What you can show is only yourself.

Your communication skill, survival skill, your personality.

The past is already passed by when you reflect

But the past should be something you can be proud of at the end of the day.

Making mistakes is not a bad thing.

Better to learn from the past and don't make the same mistakes ever again.

Live smart

Everyone is working so hard in their own way.
Everyone is in a different path.
Everyone is different but unique and special!!

You can imagine or insinuate but
You can never know what their whole story is.
You can just imagine.

The smartest people focus on what they do.
They keep moving forward and never look back.

The confidence can make you stand out
The confidence comes from self-love.

The now matters.

The reality and ideology are two different things

I have a little bit of ego mind still.

I am still figuring out to be completely at the moment like a monk.

You try not to get rid of it because I cannot, but I can accept it and face it.

You choose to be happy, breathe, smile so I have a bright next phase.

Everybody has a different way to appreciate now

I might have a different way to appreciate the now from the majority.

I notice that I simply like keeping myself busy.

I know what kind of person I am.

I feel happiness in busyness.

Being busy doesn't mean I am not embracing the moment.

That is the way I appreciate the now.

If you could embrace every moment unfolding, you will be forever fulfilled.

How to enjoy the now?

No matter how busy you are,
you keep concentrating on what you do now.

You just work on what is in front of you.

You always get sometimes in a day when you can get your mind off and unwind.

If you are concentrating and tackle some toughest one, others naturally flow and pass quickly.

Wherever you are

The place you work the place you appreciate someone.
It is all in your heart
What place or what time you do
Does not matter

The shift in the world

On the street
I can see their shoes stepping forward.
Everybody has their regular life, study, work, errand, childcare
Very similar
You are the one of them.

Life just keeps unfolding.

What kind of life do you want?
When can you have?
Do you want to have a happy life?
Actually, nothing is granted.
You can now make you happy
You have that power now.

The value of 30m

We are all given the same amount of time

You can donate time, which is a legitimate great donation

The value of just 30 is entirely up to how you spend

When you are busy in 30m or when you are lazy

When you are in a rush in 30m or chatting in the bed

Those 30m value differ

Each time has same value

You always use wisely to make your life better.

All deserve to be there

You live your life.

You can breathe. You have a right to be there.

You cannot do anything for your loved ones but you can just wish them for the best from your heart.

Those who did great deserve to be there.

Just appreciate them.

Those who did bad deserve to be there.

You don't have to get bothered.

<u>You deserve it.</u>
<u>You earned it.</u>

Every day is a blessing.
Every day you get evolved.
Every morning you feel different.

I felt down
My alarm was going off and was being snoozed

I felt so down
I did have a fair amount of good sleep but
I could not get recovered

When can you do now?

You have the most power now

Now you should do it
My belief is myself
It is what I can count on
Believe in myself
Be confident
Keep making myself pound

Make the most of your day.

Don't leave a day until you finish your work.
Don't call it a day until you get them done.

The power of NOW

Time goes by a blind of an eye on the universe scale.

You should breathe more.
And enjoy your life on your own pace.

We are the one selected to be on the globe to experience the hardships and grow into a better person.

Life is not always like fairy tale, but the reality creates a real purpose that we are alive.

Tell Thank You now

When you think you want to appreciate someone.

Time is now.

They might not be there when you really want to tell.

Chapter 3

The Power of Inspiration

Inspiration

From nature, the society, the universe.
Inspiration comes from the outside
Motivation from yourself

Humans forget so it is very important to remind yourself
of what brings you joy or pleasure.

What makes you get out of your bed?
There is always something to learn every day.

You get evolved everyday every moment.
You can absorb as much as you want.

There are full of information.
You find more when you are open-minded.

Tips: you can take journals, records, make albums, vision board.

Don't get afraid of success.
The more motivated you are, the more you can grow.

Making a vision board is one option

What inspire you?
What gets you out of your bed?
What gives you goosebump?
What gives you adrenaline rush?

Think about what inspires you.
Constantly remind yourself of what gives you inspirations.
Being aware of them makes a difference.
Everyday there is always something that awaits you, specially this age where there is overflowing amount of information.

What are your everyday goals and long-term goals?

The more specific, the better and more likely you can manifest.

What do you want in life?

Part 1 Daily joy
Part 2 The universe and nature

Part 1 Daily joy

Inspiration is energy coming from the outside
Motivation comes from the inside you.

When you get outside, you feel the energy
From nature
And from others who as well work hard

Those who sweat and tear for someone

They look desperate to me and serious in any way

The good attracts the good
The bad attracts the bad

The similar qualities get together.

Important than you accept the feeling and change it into your
energy, inspiration, motivation.

Every day is a blessing.
There is no such thing as boring in this world.
The world is full of information.
You can get out of your bed,

Randomness creates irregularity and imperfection which
creates miracle.

EXPECT THE WORST, HOPE FOR THE BEST

Everyone works for the moment, the instant moment, the one opportunity

Like your exam, presentation, even the regular fitness.

But what really matters, fulfils you, are how you spend now.

Whatever the result comes up,
It is parts of the life lessons.

The feeling of distance, connectedness.
This phenomenon

The head and the heart disconnect sometimes.

Humans act more emotionally the logically

The head tells you what you should do, and the heart tells you what you do

<u>You inhale as much energy of the world as you can</u>

<u>You can forever get inspired and get motivated in the process</u>

The love of books

They are the paradise of wisdom.

The kingdom of books.

Lots of inspiration and discovery.

They are eye-openers.

I like the touch, the size, the texture of the book.

A joy of books

I didn't understand why people can laugh while reading books.

But I do now.

When they relate to the story, when they found something interesting, they laugh.

It could be a laugh of funny, or interesting.

Music

Choose your main theme songs and choose your right songs match your moods.

How to be happy

1. Be proud of you
2. Be confident
3. Find your inspiration
4. Have a goal
5. Never lose the hope

Make a day-to-day goal to achieve a day and keep consistent.

Food

The best seasoning is the hungriness.
The little pleasure is the real pleasure

Appreciate the little joy

the daily pleasure you get are the most precious and they
are all.

Those little pleasure could be gained by your stoics
The real stoics are sensitive
They can emphasize and they could be sweet to people

The power of things

If you are stay away distant enough, you will lose it.

The inspiration in the cycle of habits

Inspiration could lose power and get forgotten as it decreases
its energy if you don't use.

However, if you do frequently in a regular schedule, you get
reminded of your inspiration in the same place or at the same
time in a day.

<u>Those way of regaining what inspire you are different for anyone.</u>

<u>Those set places and time in a certain daily cycle give you a sense of relief as those seem to allow you to be there.</u>

Learn about what is going on in the world.

That is part of your contribution for achieving world peace.

Currently, there is a fight between Rosia and Ukraine.

Bad history should not repeat.

Humans have made mistakes, but we should learn from the mistakes,

We don't want to be ugly.

Wars should never happen.

Wars are about egos, hatred, competitiveness.

Wars destroy everyone that were involved.

Wars are the definitions of stupidity and absurdity.

it is the governmental decision.

We citizens just keep worrying.

I give the biggest condolements and wish that it doesn't not make any more casualties.

'Expect the worse, and hope for the best'

Start from knowing the issues.

The first step is always to know.

Appreciate what you already have

They say,

The next neighbour's grass looks bluer.
Your grass then looks beautiful too.

What is more important than the special occasions or expensive things is what you have now.

The laughter in a conversation.
The warmth of love
The sense of belonging

You can breathe as much oxygen as you want.
You can walk with your feet set on the ground
You can feel the gravity of the raindrops
You can see, you can hear.

Appreciate what you have and know that that is enough.
So your life grows bountiful as your mind does.

The more you can appreciate what brings you pleasure from
your everyday life, the more you become liberated.

Part 2 The universe and nature

The power of inspiration the universe and nature

I feel happiest.

I feel alive.

I get motivation.

The naturists are extraordinarily beautiful.

The nature never lets our expectation down.

When you feel sad, you look up.

The universe is a key word in spirituality.

They are always with us in any age.

They are great inspiration.

My habits every day is to see night views.

They are absolutely stunning.

Cloudy day

In the morning, the town is quite with less people.

People start working form the late morning in my town.

I usually go to the café and wait in the line once it opens.

There are not as many people around me for a few hours, then when I get my works down, get out from the threshold, there are a crowd of people wondering.

This is just a small version of the world.

I can see the love, chaos, thoughtfulness, and liveliness.

All are parts of the world.

I see the positive part and contribute to those.

So, your life is brighter.

Blessing in disguise.
Light at the end of the tunnel
The silver lighting from the cloud.

The beauty of the world

They are unbelievable amazing and look magnificent.

The sky looks frosty

I cannot believe it. the more you content, the more beauty in the world you see.

I get anxious when I am happy, but I try to choose to feel much/ enough positivity and stay happy.

Because of course there are no troubles that disturb me at the moment.

It works lucratively if you are happy and work on things.

The nature is so great that they give me a tremendous amount of great energy when I inhale the air with those visions, which is such an unexplainable feeling, but feels real and great.

The more tired you are, the more you are ABLE to absorb.

You cannot when you take them as normal.

The universe is the very key term in any spirituality.

They are so much bigger than we think so we can never embrace enough, but you can apricate you're feeling when you are at them.

I am now in a naturally very blessed environment. There is not as much pollution as the previous place I was in.

There is no high building whatsoever, but they rather have hills and brick small houses covered by the British ivy leaves and the moss.

I always feel this overflowing feeling in my heart that I cannot ever take in.

They impress me.

Wherever in the world.

There are so many beautiful spot modern or natural in the world.

Traveling makes us bigger as a person.

I always desired to be a bigger person who can endure any difficulty and good at dealing with those stuff.

They are all my great inspiration.
I realize I get more when I am happy.
Happiness grows your success.
NOT success grow your happiness.
I painstakingly do think so.
I am a big fan of the nature in my place.

I am not in the southwest England.

It is a naturally blessed place.

You would notice there is no high buildings, just hills spread out.

You can see birds flying in the group,

They always enlighten us, seeing them flying so free-spiritly,

I have some energy spots.

They could not be necessarily everybody's thing, but the sport out of my house.

The sky shines no matter the weather,

the cool and fresh clean air welcome me.

My house is surrounded by the pine tree.

They are perfect to me.

They energize and encourage me.

The spot where I can see through the university in my area.

The spot on the way to the downtown connected to the long way.

There is ae so many spots to give me energy,

I feel refreshed renewed, and never let me down.

I always go beyond my expectations.

That is the power of nature.

The green nature, the blue ocean, the space is what you cannot go against whatsoever.

They are uncontrollable, look spectacular and extraordinarily beautiful.

When I first arrived at the England,

The BEAUTIFUL STUNNING sunrise welcomed me. I remember so well.

The sky

Look up the sky.

The world is extortionately big.

People have had ambitions in all time.

You can be you.

And that is enough.

Sky which is frosty and very cloudy just lots of cloud I found that I can describe like an emotion that is not sure about something and that was beautiful too this is part of the process

The power of the sun

The sun is the gift from the god.

The sunset, the sunrise

The sun in the morning, in the noon, in the afternoon.

The sun is warm and always embrace you.

The bird

The ultimate symbol of freedom.

The birds are amazing.

Did I just notice how great they are before?

Or Did I just always look down so I could not see?

They look confident.

We never understand what they feel, how they think,

The altitude where they are is different, so the perspectives change

I like looking at birds flying in the sky free-spiritedly.
They go straight to where they are going for.
I also have a sense of strong cooperation in a birds' group.

They look innocent and carefree.

We never know how they feel as the altitudes where we live are different.

The perspectives to see the world through is different.

The sound of birds which you think are beautiful could be their cry.

When I looked up and saw the birds in the vast sky,

I thought I would like to keep as free-spirited a mind as birds
while keeping as solid a will as the soil I am now standing on.

Robin
"It is enough
To smell, to crumble the dark earth
While the robin sings over again
Sad songs of Autumn mirth.

To see the world in a grain of sand.
And a heaven in the wild flower.
I hold infinity in the palm of your hand.
And eternity in an hour
A robin red breast in a cage
Puts all heaven in a rage

A turn or two I will walk
To still my beating mind."

Breathe and live.

Inhale more oxygen.
I won't get less.
There is still plenty of it.

The air

The freshness of the morning air wakes me up.
I feel brisk.
It never let my expectation down.
No matter how I feel in the morning,
I make me feel fresh and helps me get ready for the day.

It is chilling, and cold, which I am fond of.

Tree

The trees in winter are not dead.
They are waiting the warm season to come so they can flourish big and surprise us.

The beauty of flowers

The flowers and trees look lively today, making me think it is officially the beginning of the spring.

They look confident. I find it just fascinating as they naturally started to bloom in the certain seasons without any help.

I like English nature.

Their ecosystem is running so well that each plant looks like living nicely.

That reflects on me like that.

I see the daisy and the yellow beautiful flower, wild daffodil mainly.

My favourites are the white daisy but the purple one in a group looks pretty too.

I feel some fascination in the ivy,

I picked up the flower and took a picture.

The yellow little pretty flower

Wherever you travel too.

You see those natural beauty but there are particular types only common in those areas.

On the way, I took a video to capture those early spring scenery so I can send it to my lover.

There was a flower on the ground.

I could not know how to feel as it looks sad or proud.

The flower sat on the ground must have been picked up by someone who had wanted to appreciate by hand.

Feel the weather

Today was cloudy.
I don't know.
But I might like cloudy days more.
It gives me a sense of comfort.
Like a permission saying that you don't need to be always
100% perfect.
You can be more relaxed.

I see rain on the other hand as tears.
Tears are the signs of human strength.
Humans were innately born with the ego, competitiveness,
and negativity.
Showing your vulnerability can be difficult for humans.
It feels like telling me that I cannot wonder, get emotional, cry.

The weather should not be a factor to change your emotions.

But I learned to see them that way too.

The power of the universe

The universe stars the moon the sun the sky are out of control
No humans cannot control them
They even ever begin to understand never
They are too big for us and they are out of our capacity
But we can lean on them naturally
If you go with the flow,
They embrace us

It might be controlling or looking at us but
We cannot underestimate it.

There might be what we call heaven
Who really knows?

There might be a god.

What is important is your belief and hope

In the world, in the chaos or in the struggle in life, you keep
hoping so the beyond gives you energy

So all ends up so well.
It all works out at the end.

<u>Tips</u>

When you get tired

1. Get a fresh air outside
2. Find a new inspiration

So, you will know if that tiredness is from your real fatigue or
laziness.

Every day, different sceneries

I take pictures every day.

I walk on the same road and take from the same place every day.

But I take photos from different angles, from different perspectives.

So every picture looks different every day.

I meet different sceneries every day and feel different things.

Today I took the pictures of the sky, the grass, and flowers.

I feel the natural power.

Today was a sunny beautiful day!

Chapter 4

The Power of ONE Focus

The Power of ONE Focus

The one thing can change you all.

Strengthen what you are good and passionate about.

It can open everything up.
If you have the one you like, it has all the doors to all.

That interest can create who you are.

It leads to your ideal life.

GOALS ARE NOT CONCURING IT, BUT ENDURING IT

The power of mastering one skill.

You should specialise something.

It doesn't matter how many skills you have,

What matters is your specialty.

Polishing the one is more important than having the multiple skills, talents, titles.

More depth than width.

More quality than the quantity.

Be as specific when you think.

If you don't know, ask!

Width and depth

You need to have adequate width growing up.

When you start working, you are most likely required to work on the death,

I would continue what I do now in the future.

But what I can work on in the next chapter of my life is deepening my interests.

I would be thrilled to see how far I can go.

Knowing the limit of yourself is part of your growth.

There are limits but they are what we are meant to tackle.

<u>ALWAYS FIGHT WITH YOUR LIMIT</u>
<u>NEVER PHASE</u>
<u>NEVER COMPROMOISE</u>
<u>NEVER GIVE UP</u>
<u>KEEP GOING.</u>

The power of one focus

You gain others knowledge in an association of your interest
You can even learn other skills using your first interest

Your curiosity and the researching skills can open your world up
You can get it all from the focus

The one decision/choice can change everything.

Because one choice is not ONE choice.

It could be your nature and it appears in many aspects of your life.

It could lead to a life-altering or fatal incident.

What you can do now is to be as conscious of your behaviour.

Unstoppable desire

If you accomplish one, you have another goal.
If you have seemed the most beautiful scenery, do you get satisfied or want more.
Clarify what you want in life.

One focus, one passion opens everything up

Everything is interconnected so if you are passionate about a certain thing, you gain all from the one.

It changes your life, after changing your personality, your interest, your carrier, where you are, what people you connect with.

All the investment will help you achieve your goals

I am good at deciding and being better off

The power of thought

Last for the moment only
You write when you come up or speak up
It should be country limited.
I think in the language
*The language refers to English

They don't care but you should.
A lot. They are tragic but very devoted to someone.
The true and genuine love.

Goals should be ambitious and big

If you accomplish one, you have another goal
If you have seemed the most beautiful scenery, do you get satisfied or want more.

I know me.
I like keeping busy and learning more, exploring more.
Do I want to keep this hectic life?
I would rather not think this is hectic. Make it normal for me and save time and mental spacer for those I love.

Because no matter how busy you are, you have sometimes you can unwind so I will fully enjoy those time.

ORDINARY life and busy life

The power of having goals

It is equal to the power of hope.

If you have a goal, you know where you are running to and you know why you are working hard on something.

It gives you a sense of security and you gain a hope in the future.

If you are lost, you wonder and feel scared.

You get easily lethargic.

But how can you have goals?

Think about what inspire you.

There must be tons of things that inspire you in your daily life,

Be conscious of those inspiration and pursue on it.

Appreciate it.

That is all that keeps you going.

Write a vision board.

Dream and desires

If you accomplish one, you have another goal
If you have seemed the most beautiful scenery, do you get satisfied or want more.

Do you want to keep this hectic life?

I would rather not think this is hectic.
Make it normal for me and save time and mental spacer for those I love.

Because no matter how busy you are, you have sometimes you can unwind so I will fully enjoy those time.

It is up to you and your choice.

Pursue your dreams

You should not do what others expect you to do

You do you

Every pioneer is the most courageous person ever

Others might disagree, but they will see how you will turn out

You might be the first person who does it in the world.

ORDINARY life and busy life

What is ordinary?

It is by my book that you don't try sit still.

I would rather deepen my life experience.

I accept my character who likes business, and, in any way, I am accepting the fact that I would resume this time.

Make more of your time inside

No matter how grilled you are outside, your room is your sanctuary.

Your room is the most comfortable place where you can be stricter to you and shoe more.

After coming back, how you can use your time and how you can react to what is happening are leading you to tomorrow.

Idiots don't get you

I know I am more mature than the age, the looks, than my family thinks.

They are in a different headspace.

As someone says, idiots don't understand you.

I am who I am because of them for sure,

They are close minded.

Everybody has different special qualities.

They are fine.

My sister and my mother are critical in a regard.

But me and my father have a high opinion of ourselves.

Coming from the confidence and the consciousness of self-value and worth.

You know who you are the most.
You know how much you can do.
You do anything to keep proud of nobody but yourself.

Prioritize your time, preserve your space

The outside, the inside.

The school and the room.

The outside and the screen of my computer, or my phone.

Points

> ➢ Count time
> ➢ Put an earphone on and listen to your favourite audio to be productive and set your mindset.

Shut down from the world the outside for a second
Unplug yourself from the world
Just be with your thoughts and yourself.
Be selfish!

Forget about it for once. Shake it off a bit.

Sometimes forgetting about the daily routine or discipline or anything,

You need to reset. You need refreshment.

Moving really helps you to concentrate

Why you get outside is to gain another fresh air come in.
The brain stimulates by being exposed in the outside,
As it is not completely comfortable

Going with the flaw if you get stuck.

Life can be well worked out.
Life goes the way it was supposed to.

Your real passion fulfils you

When you are focused,
You don't get hungry.
You don't feel sleepy.
You even get reluctant to go to restroom.

Your lack of effort will be revealed if you stop doing long enough

If you are goal driven and appreciative about each and every moment, every day, you will be surely successful.

How to appreciate what to love

The more overwhelmingly you love something, the more you can pour love to it.

If it doesn't feel enough, you make your commitment toward your love of something stronger.

Turn inspiration into your determination and motivation. Use your inspiration as a reminder to make it in long-term.

That is your contribution to what you love.

THE SKILL THAT COMES NATURALLY IS YOUR REAL GIFT AND ASSET.

Chapter 5

Remind Yourself

Chapter 5 Remind Yourself

Part I Your memory

Memory

You forget but you remember too

Taking notes helps you remember and helps the mess sorted out

The more you put them in your mind, the more they last

It is all worth it.

The more you push the more you grow
The more you think the smarter you become
Your body your brain is honest
Your efforts is nothing but magnificent that you can rely on as
your assent in the rest of your life

The power of thought

Last for the moment only.
You write when you come up or speak up.
It should be country limited.

People forget

We need a reminder.

Reminders can be post-it or notes on PC.

The best reminder is your mind.

My way is to constantly record and take notes on my journal.

At the end of the day, what you want is a sense of accomplishment.

Count on your first impression

Appreciate what you have now and make them effective using your creativity.

What do you get when you recall your old memory?

The impression.

Good bad

Happy or sad

Blurry maybe mostly

What you can only be sure about is that.

You can get it just a second and no need to consider more.

If you want to think, you are making things worse.

Taking notes on a piece of paper and making it visual might help you clearer that.

Bet remember you don't need to think about it.

Even if it hurts you kill it, so you can move on.

Without biting your lip, you take as deep a breath as possible.

You know what will happen next?

You come up with the idea long later and feels small.

By scarifying in that regard, you make a space for others and create kindness in you.

Be strict top yourself and kind to others.

The ideas do last long

It only lasts for some second.
You do when you come up before you forget.
Important to take action when you come up.
That is the most powerful time.
That is the time things have got the power.

If you let go, you should make your mind that it is already gone, unless you are lucky.

How to remind yourself

1. Take a journal
2. Take a photo
3. Record yourself
4. Take a video
5. Use post-it
6. Create an album
7. Make a vision board

Before you forget, you always write or speak to express your thoughts.

Part 2 The importance of daily routine

Be conscious of your timeline more

5-7pm You start getting tired. Be more conscious of time

7-9pm Time pass more unconsciously although you try

9-10pm Time just passes by the blink of my eye

11-12pm You do the final rush toward the end

How do you recognize you are now at this moment?

You remind yourself and say to you
Now you are here.

Points

Sleep well and wake up early in the morning.
Be in a regular cycle.
This is the foundation of your success.

Your focus on the level of the buddha

You open your eyes, you see the entity of the society
You see the whole
You are still

You are uncontrollable by others
Your heart is solid
You see the core of everything

Part 3 The importance of sleeping

The significance of sleep

Uncontrollable human body.
I cannot fight with sleep deprivation.
You need to have a tight and long enough sleep.

Point

> ➤ Make a routine
> ➤ Should not see your phones so much after you turn
> off the light as the body knows it is the time to sleep
> ➤ Make yourself tired enough to sleep so you can sleep
> tight

The power of equality sleep.

Squeezing the energy 100% in a day and sleep tight.

You will be reloaded with a new self.

Before you sleep

The bed could be a sacred place, as you are facing straight to the sky.

So, they are getting so much power from the beyond while you are asleep.

Tips

- Say some positive words to yourself, tell yourself you are enough
- While you close your eyes and meditate, you should decide what you will do the next day
- Remind yourself several times what time you will get up
- Get ready for the next day where you will start over the same routine

Every morning is the fresh start.

So, you need to be ready to start over the same routine next day each night.

You keep evolving.

What makes you get out of the bed in the morning?

When you are tired, I could be very tough to get up.

If you are content and have some time to keep moving to, you can wake up better.

You feel freshness in the morning.

The morning has the most power because you have more energy.

Simplicity

The white colour makes the atmosphere clean and simple.

Simplicity is the beauty.
Make less, make more.
Be a minimalist.
Keep it simple
That is the best

I got grandparents who keep things all, so I understand how important to keep.

In this generation, you can make yourself beneficial with less stuff.

Now the society is getting changed and rather get an idea of simplicity.

There are a greater number of people who appreciate the humble lifestyle.

Wasting money and using money are different things.

You use it wisely. That is always the key.

Simplicity in any regard is clean and beautiful to me.
I got this insight recently.
I value this feeling.
I can take more from it.
You gain more.

The life is full of ingenuity.

You are sensitive but you can control your emotions.

And you are capable of trying to understand others hurt.

If you are stoic, your life seems easier.
Stoics are discipline.
You control your emotions regardless of situation.
What you see in front of you is not the crowd of people
You see where you go to.
You see what to do.

Your stillness pulls you together.
You are still then you are ready to up against anything.

The tomorrow is the hope

Be punctual at the bedtime.
And make yourself ready to gain a joy in the morning.

Believe that tomorrow is going to be better and beautiful
Having a faith does make a difference.

A new day

EVEVEYDAY IS A BLESSING.
YOU LEAVE A DAY WITH A BETTERSELF
WITH SOMETHING NEW

When I stand on the exactly the same spot you did yesterday,
I feel different,

I was more confident than yesterday.

The power of thought

It does not last for a long
You write when you come up or speak up

The ideas do last long

It only last for some second
You do when you come up before you forget
Important to take action when you come up
That is the most powerful time
That is the time things have got the power

Memory

I remember.

I lived in those moments.

Those vivid memory remind me of my existence. Feels relieving because I still remember it!

I am now in the café and typing this.

I feel the time passing by. What can you see? What are you thinking? The less concentrated I am on the screen, the more loudly I hear the outside or the surrounding noise.

But I like myself who is sharply focused on what I do.

How to capture a moment

You can always capture with your heart.

Your eyes are the best camera.

The more you feel sometime from it, the longer it is kept in your head.

The power of taking notes, recording, taking pictures.

They let us remember what we almost forgot.

The significance of a quality sleep

I could be hopelessly selfish when I am lying down on the bed.
Because you are still in the sleep or in your dream.
I could be in the same state on time management.

If you get anxiety, have a plan. Have a goal. So you will feel better.

Getting a fresh air getting out always helps you get out of the state.

If you are in a same room, in a bed for more than 12 h,
Your brain starts to think repeatedly,
It gets hard to get out of those thoughts.

You forcefully stop them temporality and engage in doing something plus so you can go out.

No matter how determined you are, if you are tired, you will be very hesitant to wake up.

You could be very selfish on the bed.

A quality sleep is more vital than you think.

You regret in the morning, but some repeat the mistakes.

What helps is the inspiration and the reminders.

Everything happens for a reason

I felt fatigued this morning for some reasons

1. I have been pushing myself which is a reasonable and
   understandable reason.
2. there was less affectionate and less amount of
   connection from my lover.

In the morning, I saw the bottle which I keep my daily letter
to my lover next to me.

After sleeping enough that I could be conscious of something, it
saved me mentally and made me feel better with a little hope.

Three timelines in a day

The morning 6am to 12am
The afternoon 12am 18pm
The evening 18pm to when you sleep

One day has 24 hours.
But you got 15-17/18h a day except for time of sleep
You divide your day into the three so you can be more conscious
of time

You cannot ever take over the time or stop it
But you can try to be as conscious as you can

The morning has the most power

Don't miss out the chances in the morning
You don't even know you are missing those as you are inside
your room
Get out and take a fresh air
And start an awesome day.

The outside is always stunning and beautiful
The morning air, the sunshine never let you down.

Chapter 6

Optimism, Self-confidence, Self-love

Chapter 6 The Three Essentials

Optimism Self-confidence Self-love

The happier, fulfilled, motivated you are, the better you do.

Prioritise yourself.
Respecting your time shows self-appreciation.

Always believe in yourself.

What do you believe?
I believe in myself.

The biggest things to fight with in the world is yourself and the time.

Don't limit yourself.
Drawing a line or getting afraid to go again others' expectation for you is the biggest shame.

Whether you notice the significance of self-love is up to you.

Love yourself.
Face the problems.
So, you see the hope.

Hope and love are primal in the world.

Part 1 Optimism
Part 2 Self-confidence
Part 3 Self-love

<u>My optimism is the gift.</u>

<u>And the luck.</u>

Part I Optimism

Turn that feeling to your determination.
Use it as a reminder to make it in long-term.

That is your contribution to what you love.

The subjective and objective perspective

What can you see when you are on the street? Do you see the front or observe the people around you?

Seeing things objectively is always important. It allows you to expand your perspectives including the invisible things when you think.

Always start thinking from YOU not I. it enables you to stop the ego related mind functionally.

What do you see me doing?

What do you feel looking at me doing this?

So, you can cultivate the imagination skills and will be good at anticipating other's behaviour.

A happy life

I would like to live at the moment doing what I can be passionate about.

I can die happily now.

I do nothing special but being myself.

Other don't care about you'as much as you think.

You can always turn the day around.

Even you kicked off your day late or got up on the wrong side of the bed,

You can always use the challenge for the opportunity.

Feeling down

Now is the chance to show.

You are always full of energy that could be too much that it stresses me out.

I can be calm and be selective at my decisions, and relaxed that I can more focus on my study.

Push yourself

I keep pushing myself until I reach the inevitable limitation as a human.

All humans are equal

They should be considered as individuals
The old and young
No matter what label they have

They should be appreciated by who they are
Not by their age

Be extroverted

You always have time you get relaxed
Always no matter how busy you are
Time you can get your thoughts off you for a while
You should make the best of your time for you and your loved one.
Those could generate subconsciously, which is inevitable to control

Always do the best on your pace.
Don't leave something for tomorrow and leave a day with one lesson.

---

*SOMEONE WHO IS GOOD AT WHAT THEY
DO IS INFLUENCING OTHERS TOO.*

Now you choose to be happy

That is the core

Wherever you are there you are.

The deeper meaning of this is that you belong to you.

You are always with your nurtured mind ready to fight with anything.

Be better off
Be accepting
And admit it

You are part of the society and influencing and get an impact.
You just keep going while feeling them.

You mind is stronger than anything.

Keep doing what you do
What makes you proud

Be conscious of your behaviour

Keep your chin up
Have a straight posture
Keep your face flexible

Stay away from the negative energy

Get your out of the equation is the most effective way.

It will come out good for you and others after all.

Make yourself surrounded by people who are positive

Don't afraid to leave the past relationships

Leave the past and past self

It is all for your growth

Make friends with those who are positive.

It might hurt leaving them, but it is part of your dicipline.

It means that you are being responsible for your life.

Powerful mantras

You are enough I just living.
You are perfect as you are.
You are trying the best and I am proud of you
You can do it!

Happiest life can be created by you.
You can only make you happy.
Be positive!!

Part 2 Self-confidence

Remember you are all special and unique.

Each person has different stories and backgrounds, upbringings.

However, the truth is everybody in the world should be appreciated the incredible value.

What you can do is to hold your spirit high and stand tall to make it stand out.

We are on the same fair ground

The greatest people have had those mental struggles and now they grow

They were born in the same state as everyone

None is smart or talented when they were born

They are talented people even those people make as much effort as they can deserve

They after all earn

When you see others achievement you should not to let your value down

What makes a huge difference is whether you could make effort and could pursue what you want in long-term.

Each character is special

Just apricate what you have.
Imagine what you have, where you are
All you have is supposed to be special
Don't seek what you don't have but appreciate what you have.
Give more appreciation to those

Willpower

Always up for the challenge
You always choose the tougher way

The confidence can delude people

The confidence let you shine through

The confidence coming from you is stronger than anything

So Strong that it can let others scared it doubt they are wrong

My way of talking is not based on the zen all the time

I admit I have the ego and selfishness
Which might sound arrogant and high handed
But I am being honest now

Your mindset now leads to your destiny.

<u>What you think will become your words</u>
<u>Your words become your sayings and doings.</u>
<u>They become your future.</u>

You can be as strong as you want

You have endless possibility thanks to the universe

You take and breathe in the beauty of nature

Look about the surrounding

<u>Can you be here?</u>

If looks ok, you focus on your thing.

Are you going to live your life comparing and worry about a others??

The success happiness t

They keys are self-love and confidence

<u>Your confidence in yourself can save you in a trouble.</u>

The smartest people

1. focus on yourself and provide the best possible time and their space for them.
2. they are specialized on their skills
3. good at problem solving
4. Not afraid to make mistakes

A life could be divided by whether you do or not.

The external and internal

Not everybody was born perfect

You can make yourself better by working out. And lift your confidence

Remember what you feel what others think can decide your confidence.

You be you

Do your best on your own way.

Grow your strength and something special about you.

The physically fit person is organized mentally too.

Admitting the limitation

There are always the inevitable you cannot control no matter how hard you try.

Recently discrimination happened to be in a decrease due to some activists.

The labels of the age, the complexation, the language.

But there is the inevitable

Something that a human cannot change even you try, those are the human body, on the contrary, you can control your mind.

The world and me, the perspective

Me on the street

Others on the different spots on the street

I can see others walking

I can think of them in anyway

We can think as long as I don't hurt them

They are also looking at me from others' perspectives.

At the end, what I got is how I think about them and how I think they think.

If is genuine thoughts, it must go easier in your mind.

You can always change your days around

There are ups and downs

There is a wave in a day

But you can always gain a different inspiration and make it a better day than your expectation.

Nothing goes as you plan but you can make it better.

Who is the winner in life?

Life keeps going and it never stops.
Right wrong doesn't matter.

The winner of the life in the world is the one who could discover who you are the most, who could love themselves the most, who could develop their abilities over upcoming difficulties the most.

The one who could believe in who they are and could patiently stay who they are.

It is about how long you can keep staying on your ground.

Being you is the greatest strength.

You be you.

Go beyond

Be on a next level always

So you can be confident enough to have a space to keep in your heart

You are worth living.
Be confident.

<u>Being happy being confident is the best way to revenge your bullies.</u>

Part 3 Self-love

Who are you?

I am who I am.

This is the way I am.

No one cannot ever bother me.

Adults even have hardest time to bother me.

The lover can bother me, in fast.

When I am on the earphone, everything sounds loud.

Sometimes, the silence is the loudest thing.

These phenomena happen to people who are depressed.

No one can touch me physically, no one can bother me.

Because I actually act lawful.

Who am I confessing to?

This means nothing but everything.

Something like nothing can change you.

Like each conversation with your lover.

You can only make you happy

What makes you happy is you.
Your life could be happiest by your perspective.

You create your own world

You can be whatever you want to be

Imagine that you are in the movie, and you are the main character in the story.

You are the one who shines inside your world.

There are their stories with their own characters

Rather than comparing, you love yourself.

Wherever you are

No matter where you are, you can be you,
You should know how to control it

The place where I would like to live.

<u>What do we live?</u>

<u>The god put us on the earth?</u>

There would be no meaning if the world is rainbow and butterflies.

<u>What do we learn from the pain?</u>

Because we want to be stronger.

<u>Why do you choose the rough way?</u>

It is for your self-growth so therefore you can gain sense of achievements and you will be liberated to be able to handle with the hardship.

You can reach great amounts of success as long as you can tolerate it.

Nobody will take away from you.

Develop your strength

DEVELOP WHAT YOU ARE PASSIONATE ABOUT

You can develop more on what you like doing.

People want something that is close but hardly achievable.

Like something at the top of the shelf.

I like the feeling that I want him.

I can if I keep working hard.

Young old we all feel the same in the morning
You feel different when you get up
When you are waiting in line, in a crowd train,
No matter how rich, luckily you are, you are in the same situation breathing the same air

We are all the same

I felt dull but the little part of me was telling me over and over
You got to get going

You turn the outside into the reminder of you being there.
If you get distracted or influenced bothered, which is natural,
If it is too much,
You are more controlled by others not by yourself.
They become impact for you.

The energy transfers energy
It carries energy

THE GREATEST PEOPLE KEEP INFLUENCING PEOPLE

**If you are not content with your life or yourself,
You cannot make others happy.**

If you want something, you can satisfy you sometimes

Because I had no financial trouble, I could fully satisfy myself.

But never become enough
You need to draw a line sometime

Be better off
You need more discipline

The limitation and the inevitable

There are some exceptional situations that you cannot help but have to admit the inevitable of the world.

Knowing who you are and accepting your limitation and trying to develop your strength are parts of self-love.

Love your external

Does your external define you?

If you are not physically fit, then you are not mentally well.

Some enlightened me.

I am not the fittest person in the world so I could believe that is true.

Do your belongings tell you who you are?

Look at your shoes.

In old days, shoes or shirts show your social status in the hierarchy.

Is it take care of or covered by the mud?

What kinds of bag do you have?

<u>What do you hold in your hands?</u>

It is true that you can see some of others' identity and character.

You can love your shell and your heart
You can accept with confidence.
If you are confident, others will treat you on the same way.

Imperfection is the perfection

Nobody is perfect.

If you think the person is perfect, you don't know him or her enough yet.

They work hard and earn the worth.

Or they are just good at covering their flaws.

Like a diamond.

Life could be imperfect which is more stunning than the absolute perfection

The diamond shines more when it is cracks.

You cannot decide your talent in the public

The reputation decides.
Reputation is the amount of trustworthiness.
You not just need to work hard but prove your worth in reality.

Appreciation to myself once again

If you are too strict on you, you forget where you are.

You started not to see

But remembering the very first feeling they get is important to remember

You are now in a place where you wanted to be

So, you are already great in the perspective from which a past self sees

Once acknowledge that you are enough

And you see the positive and negative influence in the similar parties

You are here handling every single day.

You are here achieving some goals in life.

It is important to push but at the end of the day, you should tap your shoulder and should encourage you more too.

The tips

yourself out of the negative equation

I left my past in the past. My friends, my memory, the
PAST-SELF

Be bold, be adventurous. Never realistic

The exceptional goes the opposite way.
They choose the tougher way and consider challenges as
Opportunities.

Prioritize your time and preserve your own space.
Your room is your sanctuary where you can do anything.
Away from the outside for a while.

The key to the success and happiness is self-love.
Love yourself and be confident.
Make the most of your time
That is how you show self-love.

Chapter 7

Manifestation

Manifestation

Goals are not about achieving it but enduring it.
Goals can be achieved by long-term effort.

The now matters. And You keep going EVERY DAY.

You feel different things every morning, so you remind yourself of what inspire you.

What gives you adrenaline rush?
What gives you butterflies?

Always seek new inspiration.
There is energy.

Prove what you can, how much abilities you have

Nobody will prove it for you, but you do.
Prove your skills and show your potentials.

Be clearer about your decisions

So, you are more likely to achieve what you envision.

Be passionate about what you do
Love what you do more

The best place to be is where you can challenge yourself

CONSIDER THE CHALLENGE AS YOUR CHANCE

Choose the plus

Not the zero, or the equal.
Always act and make something.
Just thinking without taking notes is waste of time.
The inevitable from your limit.
Don't think, move your hands.

Be conscious of what you can benefit from what helps you move forward.

Get more insights from what the areas I am not familiar with

Go beyond the limits
Handle the pressures

Points

> ➤ Get away from the negative energy
> ➤ Prioritize your time and preserve your space

Chapter 8

Discipline

Chapter 8 Discipline

First you should know what is in your control and is not in your control.

What is in your control is yourself, your mind.

What is not is the time, the universe, the inevitable, your limitation, and others' mind.

You can just assume.

What you often worry about is what You think they think. You never know what they think.

How much you can set your mind in peace hangs on whether your life goes well or unwell.

Being yourself is the greatest strength.
You might want to compare but it is impossible.
Everyone has a different measure.

The smartest and strongest person is good at self-regulation.
They keep looking at where they are heading for.

Nobody cannot take away your mind, or the knowledge.
Your mind is solely your asset.

So cultivating your mind or brain is the most fortunate time.

You try not to see what you cannot control and therefore what you end up wasting your precious time on but do what you can do now.

Discipline

Self-control that prevents from distraction and
Self-discipline of your desires and emotions are essential.

Part 1 The importance of self-control
Part 2 The importance of consistency and discipline
Part 3 The discipline in money/time management

Part 1 The importance of self-control

Are you controlling you or being controlled?

You are the one who is controlling you.

You are the one who is navigating your life.
You are the one who is designing your life.
You are the one who is steering your life.

Being who you really want to be is the strongest person
They are keeping their ground no matter what
They focus on what they do
They keep going no matter what come in their way

Rather comparing, you confront yourself.
Don't set your limits.
Always fight with your limitation.
Be the best version of yourself.

The discipline of all

You should know how to resist doing something you tend to do.

You know the limit.

Never hope.

Discipline, duty, resilience.

Completing a mission is not accomplishing but enduring it.

When you are excited or too much energy, you need to control you

You turn the music down, take the earphone off,

You once take a dep breath you get more conscious of your behaviour.

You consciously look around and become cautious of it.

You also should know the discipline of your interest

If you love something, it is harder to stop doing but

The way you can appreciate those is to keep it for the later activity too

Make the change a better one.

The discipline of your desire

You need to keep focused EVERY SINGLE DAY

You train yourself not get distracted by your thoughts and others.

That is daily stoic.

<u>Key things to achieve your long-term gaols</u>

 ➢ **Day-to-day achievements**
 ➢ **Daily consistency and discipline**

Be focused.

It is my determination and self-love

What you want to keep

Fight with your limitation and the passing time

Humans cannot take over times but
We can be conscious of the passing time.

Try to be as conscious as you can.

You can never achieve 100% of your day goals.

But you can always try to achieve 1000%.

The discipline of your desire

One top is to process once instead of acting it by impulse.

The persistency of the stoic

No matter what obstacles you face, they deep down know where they go should go to and hate giving up.

Even though they emotionally got devastated.

The smarter people live in the now and a day only for 24hours.

They are new selves next day.

Tomorrow should be a hope and a day of possibility.

Don't push the emotions

It gets worse.

They need to be convinced and eased out

You need to listen to them first and give them right solutions.

How much it means the connection with
him is

Each word of him makes me reconnect with him. They reignite the little flame.

The flame never gets gone as I keep the constant reconnection.

You control your mind

You should not even try to regulate your mind.

I feel frustrated when I notice my innocence and luck of knowledge.

Misunderstanding and misconception.

I try not to give the feeling to others.

I hate to put myself around the minus environment.

Your focus in life is about where you put your mind on.

You can only control your mind
No one will take that away from you

Don't get afraid of making mistakes

The greatest people have had those mental struggle and now they grow.

Some are not conscious of how much they do but they are doing it.

The past fades so you forget your effort.

But there you were.

If you had made mistakes, although better to take them as life lessons,

You should make it new from this moment.

Don't set your limitations or boundaries
Don't draw a line for your success

Be capable of handling the stress and pressure

If you are doing well, you need to be able to handle the stress, pressure coming from your expectation and form others.

Face the problems in front of you first

If you are not doing well, and feel anxious, eliminate the slacks one by one.

Don't hold on to one thing for too long

If you get any negative or destructive thoughts for your study, get out of there.

Go refresh or reset your mind.

If you feel hesitant to be away from them, focus on what you immediately have to do and do anything to get out asap.

Don't focus on only the outcome

Most of the things you work on are long term.

You need to be resilient.

Care more about the process and what you could have done today

Rather than your result.

IT IS NOR A SPRINT, IT IS A MARATHON.

Stubbornness or persistence?

Whether you grumble or now, you are still sticking to what you could not do at first.

Is that your stubbornness or your persistence?

If you really want to achieve something,

You should solve your problems instead of grumbling about it.

Be strict on yourself, be kind to others

By not doing what I urge to do, I can abstain more discipline and can be kind to others and to even myself.

It is simply because I suppress my impulses or the urge to want something less, the more I can give some reward when I need.

Everyone is on a different stage in their life

Not doing what you think they should do doesn't necessarily mean they are not doing what they should do.

They got different life experience and they are managing in their own way as good as they can perform.

They might be taking the shortcut or detour.

But they are their way. No cannot blame and should not.

The real strong person must be kind and can give a smile or favour unintentionally.

That is the next step I would aim for.

The journey to know who I am more.

Know who you are

As you grow, you will know more about who you are.

Make each second meaningful and even more valuable.

Sending a message, googling something, replying to someone in a meeting.

You can do it in a second.

But nobody cannot do it so flexibly.

It is their decision.

You have a right to decide.

What matters is how you take those.

The mindset connects to anything you do.

You could challenge yourself and take it to the action
or try not to do those as you are procrastinating
each action reflects your mindset.

whether you can do those small things, or you decide not to,
you are making who you are now.

The mindset can make you organized or disorganized.

Your mindset will tell you what you should do.

So, the surroundings are being changed by it massively.

Choose the opposite ways

If you want to be different, you do different things.

Your strictness, resilience, pursue, commitment on something leads to the final outcome.

All of your effort will pay off.

Nothing is meaningless.

<u>Don't be reasonable</u>
<u>Don't be realistic.</u>
<u>GO for it.</u>

Never compromise

If I compromise my thoughts, I would rather do even I am in public.

I prioritise my time rather than what others think.

They don't care.

It will soon be the past from which I will be looking at yourself.

The most important time is the now.

Keep polish yourself

I believe that life is about polishing up yourself.

Nobody was born with a perfect self.

You are you going to polish a diamond

You gain pleasure from the process of polishing yourself.

You keep polishing it.

you can be a shiny and confident diamond.

Control your speed flexibly

LEARN TO WALK BEFORE YOU RUN

You cannot go fastest in public.

Remember how to compromise you.

Nothing goes as you had planned outside.

What is important is to try to keep focusing on what you do while keeping the mind open to the outward.

Keep your direction straight.

If you are really good at controlling, you can slow down when you need.

That is even better if you could use the compromise into the stronger determination to do something when you are only with you.

Being stoics enables you appreciate small things more.

Your discipline can allow you to slow down

What if I am going to live a live with bout caring about others?

What is going to happen.
I believe that it will be easier.
Because I will do what I think is right and nothing can affect me.
And I will see how much I can handle.
Because that is my life, I am leading

That will be very fun and liberating and I will be able to be liberated a lot.

Discipline in all

A discipline in Happiness
A discipline in excitement
They all apply.

Your heart should be still at all times.
You should never step off where you once reached.
You stay on your ground tight wherever you are, whenever you are.

The more you do, the better you get

Everything in life works out well.
The skills you gained in the past unexpectedly become a great
source.
Everything you do will help you.
Everything is a life lesson.

The more you do, the more you gain.
The more you do, the more you have,
The more you push, the faster you grow.
Everything is on this rule.

GO BEYOND
Fight with your limits

When I look some celebrities or models who look confident
must be in a different state from the one you think they have.

They are capable enough to handle their feelings and the pressure
from others, so they are now they're seeing those sceneries.

They don't let the reputation fool them or let them look
miserable or dissatisfy you.

The smart people never stick to the past. They predict at all times and keep moving.

That is the next level you should aim to be.

They are seeing the different scenery.
They are already seeing the next step.

<u>Always try to go beyond.</u>
<u>Be bold, adventures.</u>
<u>Go for it.</u>
<u>Don't let anything in your way.</u>
<u>Keep doing what you love.</u>
<u>Be curious, ask questions.</u>

<u>Have as big a goal as you can.</u>
<u>Dream big!</u>

Part 2 the importance of consistency and discipline

The power of consistency.

Do it constantly every day.

Rome was not built in a day.

<u>Do you see the light when you close your life?</u>

Imagine there is a silver lining when with your eyes shut.

You should pursue something toward it.

The light at the end of the tunnel.

The lining out of the cloud.

The control of negativity

You need this skill to keep the consistency of whatever you do.

Fear is naturally coming up

Humans should not stick around it.

They are natural phenomenon but

They rarely actually happen.

You should control those feelings and try not to think them.

You need much self-control and willpower to achieve your goals.

Part 3 The discipline in money/time management

Money and time are the worth.

The smarter you use them, the more your value goes up.

4 ways to use your money and time

1. Use
2. Invest
3. Waste
4. Save

Money management

Financial independence can be set when you officially start working.

You are no longer dependent on your parents or any other supports in any kinds.

Even if you are a mature person almost like an adult,

The financial security comes last most of the cases.

The value of money.

Think about what you need

And what you want and eliminate the unnecessity.

The smarter you are, the less you possess.

Why?

What you utilize in your everyday life is actually this little amount.

You can keep the others in your heart or your head.

You can also use the device or convenient PHYSICAL material to keep them smart.

Investment

I am often urged to use money for my investment.

I believe I used them worth me or which will be worth.

I doesn't not appear the result now, but I can see it through by instincts.

Investing money on something is the key to success to in a way that you try new thing and from that you gain a new insight.

The less is more

It is not about what you get, what you gain from it, and how you use it.

You need prioritize your needs.

You need to have a clarity in your needs.

Be a minimalist

If you got one, you need to throw away one.

Simplify your life.

I have a quality life.

The value of time

The value of time is always the same.

We are only given 24h a day.

Sometimes it looks less important depends on where you are.

The equation I could be trapped in.

But each second has the same value.

Time has the same value with money.

Later or now?

<u>When are you going to do that??</u>

Only now in the chance.

The slow and the fast time

I do appreciate it but when I look back the past, feels fast.

But then I am proud of what I did and who I am today.

I am the strongest ever in my life.

I am now the best version of myself.

The switch of mind.

It is primal to switch my mind a moment something changes.

I have particular moves to make it happen. Physically, mentally, internally, spiritually.

Like a working mom.

They must be too sweet o to them.

But then three get to know how to deal with it.

Everything is about disciplines to me with a bit of empathy to others

Those are masterworks.

<u>The key points are</u>
<u>DETERMINATION, CONSISTANCY, DICIPLINE</u>

The past is the past.

The past could be the source of the confidence.

The long-term goal and consistent effort can be something you can look.

How the process goes

The start is pressure.
The middle goes fast.
The last is patient.

Those are how I feel in the race.

The worth of Money Time and You

The more you save your money and time, the smarter you use them,

The value of you goes up.

Clarify your needs

It is not about what you have, but how you use it, what you gain from it.

Freedom and responsibility

As you grow, you get more freedom with heavier responsibilities.

You get to know them in your daily life naturally.

That is why the majority for a reason the majority find the higher education more fun.

It is an exchange of freedom and responsibility.

I thought I was good at managing it. But I could be a bit unrealistic or reckless on using money.

I justify the action thinking it was investment, which you don't so frequently.

Limitations can set you free.

If there is a time limit,
It seems there is less freedom but
Humans like this.

<u>If the life is immortal, how you feel?</u>
<u>You get to be a bit scared, don't you?</u>

I am.

It takes all the purposes and meanings in life.

There is a GOAL so you can try your best to reach.

The freedom is equal to the amount of responsibility and the MUCH limitation

When I use money, I use it either use or investment, waste except for save.

No matter how much it is, I see each thing

Themselves.

They are for me the reminders of when I bought them in what state I bought.

The less money you use, you are smart.

Because the money is the gold and the worth.

You always try to use it when necessary.

The rich are good at using money

The less money you use, you are smart.
Because the money is the gold and the worth.

They know what they need.
They only use money on what they need.

It is not because not wanting to use money but because prioritizing their needs.

The subjective and objective perspective

What can you see when you are on the street?

Do you see the front or observe the people around you?

Seeing things objectively is always important. It allows you to expand your perspectives including the invisible things when you think.

Always start thinking from YOU not I. it enables you to stop the ego related mind functionally.

What do you see me doing?

What do you feel looking at me doing this?

So, you can cultivate the imagination skills and will be good at anticipating other's behaviour.

Enduring means how much you can stick to those.

Loving yourself means you respect your time.

EVERYTHING CAN BE CHANNGED BY HOW TO
SEE IT.

Take the challenge as opportunities.

Turn your fear to inspiration, motivation.

Chapter 9

What is Life?

Life

Believe in yourself
Believe always that you can do it.

We need a hope in the world.
Hope keeps you going in the world.

Part 1 The passing time
Part 2 Human communication
Part 3 How to deal with negativity
Part 4 Social Media ~How to survive this modern age~

Part 1 The passing time

What do you believe?

I believe in your family, your friends, yourself.
It is all you can count on in this world.

I believe in the stars and the moon.

It is the feeling that I am part of something so much bigger than myself that you will never ever begin to understand.

It is something that you cannot control, no matter how hard you try,

What is life about?

Life is held together by choices.

One after the other.

All shapes and sizes.

Right or wrong, does not matter.

Because life just keeps unfolding.

It won't wait around for you.

If you sit still, it could pass you by altogether.

   - The choice

People change as they grow.
The relationships with people or your preferences to things.

What are your ultimate goals?

My ultimate goals

1. To make my family happy
2. to be successful in my carrier.
3. To have a best friend/equal which is my soulmate eventually.

In the future I am thrilled to have kids and have my own house with a beautiful house.

They are my dream but actually ultimately everybody wants, and everybody feels excited about it, don't you?

What is the purpose of life?

Life is about discovering yourself.
No one was born perfect.
No one can ever come to the absolute perfection.
You go over and over the limitation you face and keep going in life.

Your life is immortal. The life keeps unfolding.
So, you never have to be afraid of mistakes.

At the end of your life, what you want is the greatest MOMENTS, not the longevity.

You might die tomorrow.

The value of 24 hours every day has the same value for everyone and every day,

If you cannot be happy now, you cannot be happy forever.

You choose to be happy.

Do you take your life dying or living?

You might not why you exist but

Your perspective can make everything positive.

What is sure is you are in control of your life.

There are some chapters in life
The more you think, the more it sounds precious, which makes me think it is going fast.
You go to the college.
You start working,
You build a family
You raise children
You enjoy your afterlife.
they are just a serious of now

Life cannot be easy
Life challenges you forever
you are now being trained so your life will be easier.

You are now discovering yourself and learning how to live with the upcoming adversity.

What is the most crucial is the intangible.

Your feeling now, what impression you got from your accomplishment, the connection you made with your loved ones.

On the way, you should never stop dreaming, hoping, believing yourself, which hugely affects your confidence and your motivations.

Who knows who gave you a life, a chance to live on the planet?

But you can feel and breath.
You should live and breathe and enjoy as much as you can.

What do you want at the end of your life?

What do you what in life?

There are so many elderly people.
They are old and cannot even walk.
It is the destiny of life.

Everybody goes dying and new life is born.

WHAT HAS A SHAPE WILL BE GONE SOOER OR LATER.

What did the old gain throughout life?

The tangible is less important than the intangible.

I can now see why my grandma loves to travel with her friends and my grandpa still continues to work.

They are the purpose living in the world.

The feeling, the sense of achievements, the impression

They are all you can count on.

As long as you are proud of you now or in the future,
you are completed the mission on the planet.

Life is

Immortal.
You will die at the end.

like is your long journey
life is for finding yourself
life is for discovering the new.
Life is to learn to live with difficulties and obstacles.

Life can give you great pleasure by your ways of thinking or processing it.

Life is about you
Your feelings.
Your achievements.

What is the good and the bad?

<u>What is it in the first place?</u>

We can never define it.

We don't know if the babies were born with a good spirit of evil.

But the truth is some got twisted or not educated nurtured thoughts, so they get defensive.

There would not be wars or any conflict in any kind in this world.

Animals don't fight like humans do.

Education or upbringing are what led them who they are mostly.

If they are not stable, they went down the wrong way.

I might make their life tougher and forced to be what you call BAD PEOPLE.

When I see those people, I don't see what they do but WHY they do.

What made them become like that.

Time

The ideal

The past is what you can be proud of
The now is what you focus on

The future is what you hope for
My friends once said,

THE AWARDS ARE SIGNIFICANT BUT TOTALITY.

*THEY ARE SOMETHING THAT SHOWS YOU DID
A GREAT JOB AT SOME POINTS IN LIFE.*

Time flies.

Life goes so you keep going,

Never compromise and never stop giving up on what you are up against.

The successful people know what they want what their focuses are.

life is about knowing about you.

Seeing your growth and gaining sense of achievements, they are the greatest gifts in your life.

<u>The busier you are, you gain more.</u>

<u>The wisest people are good at what you do.</u>

<u>The clever people consider risks opportunities</u>

I feel the slow and the fast at the same time.

Part of me doesn't want to think in a way that I mind the timeline.

I live each moment in the moment so I can always be happy.

You should be more conscious of the time flow.

It is going quite fast, which means that you are centred on what you do, and you are enjoying in the day-to-day life.

What makes you feel different is your growth since you EVERYDAY get evolved.

You become a new self every single day.

Never go back, never look back.

I used to think what the life is about.

Now I know well enough, I believe…

I would describe like this.

Live a busy life

<u>Which life would you prefer?</u>

A life with longer longevity but less qualitative or a life with shorter but more qualitative.

I would choose the latter.

Because you cannot sit still for a long.

You have to work and make ends meet.

So I would like to make a busy life less busy.

Real happiness is invisible

Love, bond, connection.
A sense of accomplishment.

Moments by moments

Life should not be counted by years
But by the moments

It will become a series of your happy moments.

Frankly when you struggle, when you are in a trouble,
You should enjoy it.

The significance of your choice

Miracles do happen by the choices you made.

Calm down, take a moment,
slow down for a second

You might see the peace, the silence in this crazily busy world.

Summary

Life doesn't go reasonably and logically.

Humans are dependent to their emotions too.

The physical well-being and the mental well-being are reversed
back one another.

<u>Never take anything for granted.</u>

Even it is less than before

Have a broad perspective.

Keep your mind open.

Put more channels on your heads.

<u>So, what can you see?</u>

The entity.

There is another entity out of the small entity.

It is **infinite**.

To conclude, life is unexplainable.
It is philosophical.

It is your challenge.
But it is up to you whether you flourish on the globe.
Up to your perspective. How to see it. How to take it.

Life could be ironic and never go as you expect.

So, your positive and forgiving ideas help you.

Again, LIFE KEEPS UNFOLDING.

TIME NEVER STOPS.

TIME FLIES.
BY THE BLINK OF AN EYE.

Nonetheless, you should keep the memory the past inside the drawer.

You were surely there.

Part 2 Human communication

Life is full of difficulties so we can use the ingenuity and cooperate with others

You affect them and get affect them which is just natural.
But what you need to do is to control.

I relax my mascle by stretching my face and the shoulder.
Try to make a positive-looking posture.

Humans can feel

Those smart people attract the smart people more.

People who are capable of appreciating and resonating.

You feel the change of emotions.

When you walk outside, I can see my change in my emotion.

Meaning that I cannot stay still and centred.

You are distracted.

But we cannot AI or robots

You care and think about others

You empathize

If you get hurt by you doing what you knew it was bad or wrong or saying bad things or lying,

You are deep down a good person.

You are a human.

<u>When you are not happy, you cannot be share.</u>

Human nature

You care, get hurt, overthink, compromise, apologise.

It might show you a kind nature.

But next time you do, you get the opposite results.

Accept the fact that human communication is complex chaos, and insane.

Be cool and casual.
Keep moving.

People affect with each other

The physically closer you are, the more you can see and get influenced

Because you can feel.

Be the positive influence.
Portray what you would like to be seen from a objective perspective.

A GREAT LEADER IS A INFLUENCER.

Do humans change?

The more you grow into adulthood, the tougher your mind becomes and the harder you can change your mindset.

What is the real difference in human qualities?

They are so many people outside.

But they might look the same for all for other kinds of animals, looking at ourselves from a broader perspective.

Due to their complexion, they look externally different which are normal.

But they look the same to me too.

The real change you want is invisible

Some consistent effort you make every day can create a huge different.

We cannot judge by the external.

We never know who they really are at the core unless you know them for a while or you begin a conversation with them.

Your trust

The trust you built up every day doesn't disappear.

Something invisible but strongly banded.

You could break down all by one mistake.

If you do something wrong, you are digging the ground and making a hole where you will fall in and

The bigger you make, the more you cannot get out. Nobody will come help you because that is your fault.

If you continue lying nobody will believe you.

Reputation and trust are built up by long-term period of time

---
ROME WAS NOT BUILD IN A DAY

Think about those worldwide brands.

They are successful as they got the trust from their history

People tend to buy those items often as they are more reliable than the other local company.

They cannot see but they get clear when people notice them.

Those are the real difference you want to make and those can make a tremendous change in the world

It is powerful although they are also same human beings

They are still stronger than AI too

Each generation has its changes

It is up to your perspective that prevents you from getting affected

What is philosophy?

It is the way real smart people think
It is not just deep-thinking
It is the clever people's ways of thinking in their daily life.

Conversation rules

Less words more meanings

'The honest answer deserves an honest answer'

1. ASK QUESTIONS!
2. Add information.
3. You listen more.
4. Make the conversation entertaining,
5. Be serious when the other person is serious.
6. Be honest.

Don't be judgemental

Everyone looks the same to me from first sight no matter where they come from.

What matters is the inside.

Their inner quality makes quite an impact in society as proven by those who have lived on their life.

You cannot tell what kind of person they are before they actually start to communicate but some little behaviour can sometimes reveal all.

Everything happens for a reason

One mistake doesn't necessarily come from the one.

Their mindset they accumulated let it happen.

Good or bad

There is not perfect or 100% match for your choice.

For example, when you walk,
You can bow or neglect them.
There is no perfect answer.
The social situation is complex.

You CAANOT act in a way that you can make others 100% comfortable.

What is important is you try to give a GOOD-LOOKING impression to others.

Part 3 How to deal with the negativity

You don't want to let that negativity that makes you look miserable and dissatisfied.

Everything is a life lesson

You make mistakes and you grow,
But I am sure I just felt down and went dark.

Pain mild

There are full of pain mind in this would more
You give you a reward
You are more likely to get you separated from them

You feel something bad ironically good, like movies.

The TV reveal more humans' ugliness

The modern world is so twisted.

The more you emersed in pain mind, the more impacts you get and the harder you get out of it.

It becomes like an addiction.

Simplicity, the ancient wisdom is now needed now.

They don't care but you should do

Do you care what others think when you do something?

When you walk
When you are sitting
When you are working on your hobby

Would you rather care about the result or the process?

I would rather care about how I can use now rather than trying to figire out what I cannot solve and end up wasting my time.

If I did impact someone in that way, let it be.

I would rather keep impacting people if it is what it takes, if it causes something just because I am living.

I would rather pursue what I want rather than sticking around some kinds of assumptions or judgements.

At all costs.

We are all busy with outlives
We don't actually care about each other as much
People get too conscious of their behaviour in a irrational way.
They don't care but you should.

Fear

Humans have fears.

We need to know how to live with it.

We should see What if, not What if.

Because most of what you get afraid of don't happen.

They have animosity about something like the other things,
the other people.

But nothing you think of is going to happen.
Live in the moment.
Stand on the ground on your feet.

Don't let fear make you feel dark.
When you face it, it is different, and you can see something.

Always
<u>Admit, face, accept your fears.</u>

<u>So, it won't haunt you.</u>

You cannot prevent something from happening for 100% guaranteed.

But you are reassuring your feeling by taking action.

When you get anxious

Focus on your day-to-day goal.
You can only live 24 hours at a time.

Take a breath
Inhale the negativities and the hatred driving you.

Think what you want

Is what you want being better than others?
Is what you want achieving your goals?

TAKE AN ACTION

If you get anxious, you breath and stretch your body and start over.

You can make a new self by a second or each moment.

The more you make the new one, the more you get evolved and grown into a stronger self.

Let your imagination drive you.

Too much worry is not necessary

Work on for the better and keep you as positives a person as you can.

HIGH VIBES, BETTER LIFE

Accepting your limits and know who you are

Knowing your weaknesses and your limitations doesn't make you weaker but makes you a stronger person.

EVERYTHING CAN BE CHANNGED BY HOW TO SEE IT.

Take the challenge as opportunities.
Turn your fear anxiety worry to inspiration, motivation.

The uncertain of my future

It might intimidate you as it is not certain.
But it has been all working out.

Everything is in your head

Like fear or insecurities

You cannot control.

So, you feel loud even when it is silent.

You might feel louder when it is silent.

Perspectives change things

Everything is perspective

Every negative thinking is never going to be the reality
Except the exception which rarely happen.

Take it easy

Life is already tough
You should not make your already difficult life even more
difficult.

Your little negative voice is your biggest bully.

Children v Adults

Adults know how to maintain their life
Children are more of a dreamer

Adults try to run their life today
Children get more passionate at the moment

Adults are more capable to keep going I've the obstacles

Adults mean how mature you are.

Children could be as smart as they are

Adults or the old look smarter

Ask questions and think why.
So you can be closer to them

There is no much difference as much as you think there is.

When you made when you are near to the adulthood

Children are more innocent, sensitive, genuine
Know the good and evil more
They are closer to spiritual world
They have different fear
They are from their broad imagination

They have more sensitive taste, feelings, heart

Adults hit the walls again and again
They are forced to be strong

But they still have insecurities and fear that are more complex.

Adults have more experience

They are masterful at living in the world

Coexisting has never been a easy thing but they learn to live

They might have been broken but they pick up what they missed and start over again.

They can act as if they were ok if necessary

They can change their facial expressions depends on the situations.

They can predict the future and are good at adjusting to any situation based on their experience.

The conflict into adulthood

The confidence makes them look like adults

They have got experience, so they know how to behave for their habit

Just practice it

PRACTICE MAKES IT PERFECT.

How to be better off and become an adult.

Adults look cool to me due to the responsible and chilling behaviour.

What I see now is ridiculous with much respect and find it similar to the way I do.

They got so much experience.

They can be kind, less sharpened.

So you can enjoy your life and you can in addition spread the positivity

The balance

Life should be balanced out

When you are too excited, you get strict on yourself.

When you are stressed, you tapped your back and let yourself relax

When you feel down, you give yourself a treat a kind word.

Don't miss the opportunity

Taking the opportunity is an ability to be successful
You might miss out the opportunity
You sometimes miss the boat
And they left you
Besides don't shut the world down

Innocence is a biggest pitfall

You even don't recognize that you are missing if you don't try.
The range of interest can widely open up your future.
That is the biggest shame.
Innocence is the last thing you want.
You never know unless you try it.

Unlock your world

Gaining more knowledge in many fields can expand your carrier choice,

The more you know about a thing, the more interested you become.

Always getting to know something is what you can do for the start.

The power of beliefs

It could be scary to lose my steadiness, stability.
There is always a thing to fight with.
Believe that you can do it.

Part 4 Social Media ~How to survive this modern age~

The modern era

This is the age of information.
It could be extremely overwhelming and overflowing,
People use Instagram or twitter, as you can name more.

<u>I always try to remind myself constantly of how I want
to use those and how I cannot be taken advantage of.</u>

Social media is a great revolution in the modern world,

The wise usage is vital.

<u>How do you use social media?</u>

In my view, this world could not be any better in terms of
technology.

It just gets escalate except for the details,

I think about what I want no matter what age I was born into,

The efficiency with enough human advance connection

The connection with myself mostly.

And now due to the technical advances, we got the complete
option.

Again, whether you have a happy and quality of life is up to you.

There is a vast amount of information.

The target is the quality.

For instance, regardless of how ambitious you are, you cannot read the entire set of books in the library.

You could be able to, but you need a lifetime to appreciate all deeply.

The point is the quality or productivity.

The balance of the speed and the amount.

What matters is what you learned from the book.

So, you extract the important information or something that triggers you.

And work on researching on your precise interests,

I want to use social media for collecting sources in a right way.

For connecting with my family remotely.

For giving a change to connect to the world.

The e-learning system could be the most effective learning style although it could be depressing in a way that there is not as fun.

You have multiple ways to get yourself out there for study, personal interests, or work,

It could be more comfortable and effective than the actual researching specially these days.

I would rather stay in front of the screen forever by connecting with people, stuck in a room if it could be my investments of time.

You never get caught up if you know the wise way.

The insecurity of social media is the same amount of the security.

It is just about how wise you can use it.

Points on not getting distracted by social media

- ➢ Decide what to do before you unlock your screen.
- ➢ Be aware of time you use it for.
- ➢ Use credible sources or only use the official sites.
- ➢ Download some important sources.

On making friends online

You can make friends from all around the world through online.

The friendship online seems lighter and easier, which makes us downplay the relationships.

Which the old generation never ever could not feel.

I value those relationship just same as face-to-face/direct contact in person.

The hardest part is it is so easy to add your friends and to erase them too that I get confused a bit with handling it.

Communication is the same.

Abrupt shut down in a conversation may hurt others' feelings.

You tell a reason why you must get going.

Lying not to give a bad impression, a bit twisted, but could be applied.

You can either read it and not reply, or don't see when you notice too.

Telling exactly the reason you cannot is kinder than ignoring it.

You can cut the conversation nicely and tell them I got to go.

That is how you should communicate; not shutting all down or putting the guard up.

You tell how you feel explicitly, as it is important in the direct communication.

What an amazing world

The social media is a window to the world.

It is what connects us even when we are distant.

Now that the technology developed prosperously.

They should not be taken in any way for granted.

The old generation must get really jealous about how great they are.

This world is quite accessible and that is the blessing.

You should not take those for granted.

In addition, you should not be taken advantage of too.

You only use what makes your life richer and the life you want.

Reignite your creativity

The more you grow, the more likely your brain is less flexible and less creative.

You can reopen your imagination through online.

There are tons of sources to use.

Educate yourself online

The smart people learn from mistakes
They get curious.
They ask questions and research.

Who should you aim to be?

The real strong person in the modern age would be someone who can be still in the busy world

Those who are mindful, nurtured, and not distracted.

They would appreciate the simplicity

I feel these days that their ways to communicate with their friends rapidly changed

The gravity of each fried is different compared to the past

You can so easily find a new friend and exchange your email just with some steps

Before, the email exchange would have meant more for them,

They can connect more but they can let go of their friends each friend.

On a positive perspective on the social media, the definition of gaming is now being changed and is taken differently

They take those as educational material
They can create a friendship there too.

The less is more

You should keep your life simple.
Simple is the best.
Less could be more.

You cannot get all.
You prioritise and clarify what you care.

Be selective

The world is full of information

So be selective and identify what you need to make your life better

What you don't need

The positivity in a conversation

What you can do the best for the person is to hope for the success, stability, the wellbeing security or safety.

You can only hope when you are away from them. Nonetheless it can give you the courage and brighten you up.

The least but the best thing you can do is to give them positive and encouraging messages.

Words convey your feelings.

Words have the effective power.

Chapter 10

Practicing zen

Practicing zen

Negativity comes from the realistic thinking.

Humans are emotional and a little too clever being.

You don't need to suppress them as the more you push, the more it pulls.

You accept your ego, and negativity and think of what you can improve on.

You do you with a bit of a compassion.

Self-love is the key to happiness and success.

It is all you can count on throughout your life.

Part 1 Practicing zen

Do you have the ego?

I have an ego.

People get attached to something: they love it so much that they don't like to share.

They see more in those who have same interest.

Just like they can see those who love the same person as them.

They get competitive and try to make the best out of it.

Calm down.

You don't have to be the one.

What you want is your best version and the accomplishment that you set for yourself.

Have you ever seen illusions people or felt the line of an eye although there is no one for real?

Because you are now so self-absorbed and cannot see the surrounding.

That causes you that phenomenon.

<u>Have you ever felt overwhelmed because you love something so much?</u>

<u>How do you cope with it?</u>

Where does ego come from?

When you are possessive to something,
When you share or give something,
When you are a competitive nature,

the ego comes up.

The egos' rules

The more you try to suppress it, the more it comes.

So just accept the fact that you have an ego.

What you have to do is to practice your mind in a daily life.

You cannot get rid of all, but you can reduce it.

The rule of your ego

The more you push, the more they pull

The more you suppress your thought, the more comes.

Mental conflicts

Uncontrollable mind.
It is not that simple to control your mind.
The more you try, the more it comes.
It is persistent and daunting.

There was something I could not get off my head
I got tempted to think about it as I knew it is unnecessary.
But it triggers me.
Ask yourself,

What do you want?

Tips

1. Put your earphones on unless it is necessary for you to be out so, you cannot get distracted.

2. Count the time
   Time is uncountable

Nonetheless
On the process, to get over the boundary you set for yourself,
Counting time helps you conscious on what you do.

Competitive thoughts

You cannot compare because we have different strengths and weaknesses and we have got a different measure to measure.

Comparison does not end, and you will never come down the answer.

If you could get your out of your competitiveness, you life becomes less busy.

<u>Are you competitive?</u>

You don't need to compare.

If you are still comparing yourself with others, you are still the same with the majority.

Egoic opposite is self-love.

If you are confident enough,
If you are on the different level,
If you are really superior,
You don't need to compare.

Train your self-control

You stop yourself from overthinking it.

Needs some courage to get rid of the thoughts and you need to be patient, but I could accept it today.

Your thoughts are based on ego

How can you know yours is egoic

Simple.

Do you compare yourself with others?

How do you process things

If you are worrying f about what others think.

Are you competitive?

Do you try to make yourself based on other opinion.

The conscious or the subconscious

You do think although you don't need to
You don't think although you are not sure.

The inevitable from your limit

Don't think, move your hands

Be conscious of what you can benefit from what helps you move forward.

It is all in your head

You decide your confidence your mind can decide
Nobody cannot decide, or you should not let them decide
It is how you take it.

You cannot get both

There are ups and downs in everything.
You should be able to let them go as they go.

When you rise, you need to expect the down.

When you eat sweet you need salt.
When you are serious at work, I want to watch comedy.

Stay away from the negative energy what triggers you down the dark place

You need reminder something that keeps that mindset

Start paying attentions to what you inspire you.

When you notice you have ego, you are now changing to be a better person.

Never suppress your feeling or blame too hard for feeling that negativity.

It is a basic human nature.

You are now on the right track of zen mind

You will never be perfect, but you can keep polishing your diamond.

Contacting with your friends

Whenever you feel you want to tell you tell.

It's does it matter when they see

They are all passed things for both parties.

Don't be judgemental

Feel it.

What makes a significant difference is not the external.

What you want for a friend is a mentally beautiful person.

Do mantras scare you or pressure you?

I get it. I do too.

It could be intimidating.

Because you don't know you can really do it.

It is ok to feel that way.

Say to yourself,

<u>You are enough.</u>

<u>The more you push, the more they pull</u>
<u>The more you suppress your thought, the more comes</u>

You accept it.

Part 2 How to think

The zen masters must see the stillness in the chaos.
As their mind is solid and steady.
They don't see others mind
They are where they are going for.

The world is a blank sheet

It could be full of ego that you have and what you create around the ego toward the surrounding people

If you are still and centred, you can paint on it and create your own world.

Can you see the light connected to the future?

Imagine it when you meditate

Your life is going to be as it is meant to be.

Everything happens for a reason.

Count on your first impression

The past what you remember consisting of impression.

What do you get when you recall your old memory?

The impression.

Good bad

Happy or sad

Blurry maybe mostly

What you can only be sure about is that.

You can get it just a second and no need to consider more.

❖ ❖ ❖ ❖ ❖

In the bookstore, in front of the shelf.

I was reading book and accidentally dropped a book off the shelf.

I am in full concentration.

But instinctively said sorry.

So the other person said it is ok

It is nice but I kept reading book.

Should I have said thank you to the person.

I care too much and figure out something which never will.

I was overthinking it after I resumed reading book.

But later there was no perfect answer for what I should have done in those situations.

Because you cannot control others mind by your action.

The best answer for it

Believe that what you do at the moment is the best for you and for others.

Just believe so.

If you want to think, you are making things worse.

Taking notes on a piece of paper and making it visual might help you cleaner that.

Bet remember you don't need to think about it.

Even if it hurts you kill it, so you can move on.

Without biting your lip, you take as deep a breath as possible.

<u>You know what will happen next?</u>

You come up with the idea long later and feels small.

What kind of like person would you like to become?

You know what is good
You do what you think is right so you can be proud

There is no best answer in human communication

You might have delusion created by your egoic imagination.

You hear something which is not there.

You see things closer to you although it is far away

You create those things because they are more conscious of yourself and not pay enough attention to the surrounding which result in hurting you

You are more protective about your body but more as protective to your mind.

Compromise

When you get out, you are part of society.

You sometimes need to compromise what happens to you.

Forgiveness

You should have a sense of forgiveness and some space in your mind that you can lead a hand to someone in need, give a nice smile and bright greeting.

Be a positive impact on society

There is no perfect answer in communication.

You just have to try to give a positive influence on people around you.

You are in the minority

Stop thinking you are the only one.

Know that the counterparts for you are everywhere

But it must be rare and, in the minority,

Keeping standing your grand and make it true

The significance of the proof, the evidence, the entitlement

Those are the valid skills which now then others start to appreciate

What is beneficial for others
is beneficial for you too

You make yourself your product beneficial for the users as much as you can

You are not fool

And they are busy and want some benefits from yours or you

The beneficial characters are appreciable for everyone

Specially those limited number of useful products start to stand out

There are some but not many

Whether you will be in those minority, it is up to your action.

Part 3 What is the next step?

You are now the master of zen
What should you do
You can share your energy to those you love trust
Those you think deserve listening to your ideas

New me

As a result of practicing zen, my mind is more opened to people, and I got more space and time to give people in need

The world could be loud and hectic but if you could make the world less noisy less busy, they can enjoy it.

They should rather appreciate the little pleasure in a regular life than they do in a special occasion.

So, their mind will be more nurtured that way and they can always be liberated and happy eternally.

Coming from each moment as time keeps going on and on.

The little joy and relief from a tight schedule are more meaningful.

The more cultivated your mental intelligence is, the more you are capable of valuing the little things that happen to you.

So you can be happy whenever and wherever you are.

I start to see the invisible.
I can see the little light with my eyes closed.
I don't see people or the buildings outside
I see just the blank white page
Nothing is painted and I see the white page where I paint.
I used to see their mind inside and surrounded by the busyness.
I have gained the stillness in me.
No noise bothers me.

I can see the future through.

When I meditate for a while, I see my focus going inward and learn to take advantage of time moving forward.

Time goes fast if you are focused, which means that the toughest time will be passing soon and it will be nothing later.

I can see the straight road connected to the future after a long serious of the now each moment.

I don't need to rush but I can expect.

Where you can challenge your zen spirit

That is when you are in a familiar place, when you are surrounded by those who have known you for a long.

Those situations really challenge you as you get less conscious of you.

The spirit of GIVE
You share your energy.

Chapter 11

What is next?

Part 1 Gratitude

The appreciation

You appreciate the nature, your family, all the environment you get influenced by and you influence.

So, your life gets easier.

The self-discipline in happiness.

You should also not forget the gratitude to people who support you directly indirectly and the consideration and thoughtfulness to care about others.

'Okagesama' a Japanese phrase
'Arigatai'

They are both Buddhism related word.

Okagesama means to appreciate people who support you on the shade on the back

Arigatai means not to take anything for granted.

They are sophisticated beautiful words.

You can a lot learn about simplicity humility and appreciation from Japanese culture.

Appreciate each interaction with your people

We are now here sharing our precious time.

Regardless of what happened in your life so far, now we are here to talk.

This could be the pivotal moment in your life.

Real kindness. Genuine consideration.

<u>The give.</u>

An interaction between strangers

Some talked to me when I was standing on the street.

He worried about me standing on a sweet alone for a long.

I was there after he was on the way back.

He cared again and asked me if I am ok.

I told him I had been messaging someone on the corner of the street and he asked me if I am ok, thou.

That is his real kindness.

When I said I am ok, he passed by casually.

That is the give.

Nice smile saves your day

You always want to share your energy and positivity.

You should appreciate every chance to get interaction with others

It is more influential to you and other than you think

Just being conscious of the points will make who you will be.

On a street

Besides the outside is full of human love if you focus on them.

Some people brighten up the city centre with their guitars or other kinds of musical instruments.

There are a couple of people who encourage them to play in front of them.

There was a man who does not have one leg, taking a child.

He looked like a stronger father than the ordinary father.

The child looked happy as he should be.

There was a mother who passed some coins to her kid so he can give a homeless man those.

Some cleaners clean up the town in the early cold morning.

Some salespeople briskly greet people without seeking returns.

There is so much love in the busy Sunday morning.

The application to small things is more important than one of the special occasions.

What gives you that pleasure, joy,

Is everything in the world.

The warmth of people.

The laughter in a chat.

The more you appreciate the little discovery in the world, you will be more fulfilled.

A peaceful world

The sky in current Ukraine is now threatened.

What gives people a sense of comfort starts with the blue clear sky.

You should never take any natural beauty for granted.

Part 2 Hope

The power of hope

No matter how tough, challenging the situations are, never lose hope

Hope is what keeps us going in life.

Never lose the faith.

Keep seeking the new insights.

The more you push to gain motivation the better your life becomes in my opinion.

Also never forget the gratitude.
There is no later in expressing your appreciation
If it is late, it is late
Life is unpredictable really.
Anything at any time comes in your way.

The power of words

Words are something you convey your feelings on.

But putting meanings and emotions with true transparent meanings is more important than anything in communication.

We are humans who went through similar life obstacles.

AN HONEST ANSWER DESERVES
AN HONEST ANSWER.

The more honest you are, the more likely you can connect with them.

I am perceptive, introspective

I am protective of my ideas.

But I would love to share to people I deserve.

The people I want return a favour to.

The people I can trust and want to connect with.

The more you share, you are reminded and aware of the importance of what you just said. And make the understanding deeper.

Never seek the give or return from anyone.

It doesn't last.

Don't take the nature privilege for granted

The skills to learn are what I do today.

Educate myself, learn the skills usurious for the future. Expand the knowledge from books.

I always like to spread the knowledge rather that keeping it in me

Be happy to the fullest

Don't get afraid to be happy smile

You can surely be happy after you are happy

You should believe it.

I hope it.

Keep being inspired

Be ambitious, adventurous

The happier you are, the better life you have.

You cannot give when you are unhappy or tired

When you are sad, down, mentally ill,

You see something different in a sunny beautiful day.

Your heart reflects on your thoughts.

HAPPY mindset can make you HAPPY.

Everything is a life lesson.

For you to grow.

Smile.

You should never forget the appreciation.

Should not take anything for granted.

What is important

Every philosopher says the same thing.

Self-love, and prioritising yourself is the key your success and fulfilment.

Discipline is needed in all things to achieve your long-term goals.

You have to resist your emotions by self-control.

Goals come true by your resistance and day to day effort.

The key things in the book were to know what is in control. Be aware of your deeds.

Clarifying what is important to you.

Additionally, adversity comes in sometime,
You just keep going!

And
Never forget the gratitude for the UNIVERSE and what we connect with, family and friends and more.

What always comes back to is the physical and mental well-being. That is the most important!

You are now seeing the right direction.

Your focus is now on what you want.

Your focus is inward.

You are seeing the different scenery, which is more beautiful than ever.

You are now ready to run straight toward the light you can see.

Last Words

No one can take that away from you.
What is important in life is the invisible the intangible
The feeling you obtain in your head

Everything hangs on the perspective

Be positive
Choose to be happy.

Remember everybody is trying hard to do the best they can
You are too

Because there is a choice of death
You normally don't choose

You have to live on
Keep going

If you are now happy, you are happy forever
Life is a series of the now

Never give up

As you grow you learn to be consistent
Which was hard as a child

Every effort you make every day will make you into a big
person.

Seek the inspiration every day

The next level of it is be happy for other

Your mind will be more free

You know what is good
Do the good

Not only does it make the world better, but you could lift your
value.

You can be more proud, and confident

You can make the busy world into a less busy world.

Have a faith.

You need practice for being resilient and eventually being
mindful and still

Humans remember them if you keep reminding yourself of
what means to you

Always fight with yourself while appreciating what you do

Not getting over the boundaries that others created but
You get over your limits

It could be your ego mind

Get over it asap and go to the next level.

Life keeps unfolding
Life is short

Choose to enjoy your life
You can only choose your happiness or unhappiness

You do it right here right now

I ask you again,

<u>What kind of life would you like to lead?</u>

<u>What kind of person would you like to be?</u>

Be clear at what you want in life

WAITING IS A VIRTUE

Always make efforts on what you want
They will come to you who waits

You will have different taste as you grow and as time goes on

You believe in the light you see inside your eyes
The real joy is inside you
Keep following the light

That is connected to your future
That focus on the light will lead you to the bright future

You have your own ways of meditation.
You can do it while you close your eyes
Lie down straight to the sky
Where you receive the privilege of energy from the universe
The bed is where you rest and be ready for tomorrow very
sacred space in that sense.

Don't be afraid of your mistakes and know what your
problems are.

If you cannot, then laugh it out.

You can just move on.

What do you believe?

I believe….
in myself.
Because that is all you count on. If you stay strong, you are
more likely to overcome the difficulties you face.

Keep wondering. You can wonder and consider. If you are born
in the planet, you are freely wonder.

Life itself is the wonder.

You live for the wonder, adventure, discovery, and for the evolution.

Reaching YOUR OWN goals in your best way means being able to see the scenery that you have never seen.

Those scenery you see is your greatest assets for your life.

They are your accomplishment.

You keep those trophies in your heart.

You are proud of yourself, and you taught you something.

You can die with them.

What is in it after you die? Yes, it is the funny part. Nothing left.

Humans are destined to die.
Humans make wars. Fight with the ego.
But at the end, we all die.

What created you with your soul? Who made the time, the conception? What about the universe?

What you want is yourself and your accomplishment NOW!!!

You can create from your daily life. There are always things you can do and get those rewards from.

There are many ways to apricate now.

My way is to keep myself busy. I gain pleasure from the business as I am now on the process to accomplish a day goal and can tell that it leads to the long-term goal.

Every day, you are becoming a new self.

Never look back.

Right or wrong does not matter as time goes on.

You keep going.

You feel fear.

You might get fearful when you are excited or succeed one.

Because you expect be the downturn

Expect the worse, hope for the best

If you feel fear when you are doing great, just be happy. Again, Enjoy the now.

This kind of fear reflect your realistic perspective, which is good. But you don't need to feel downward.

You look up every single time. HIGH VIBES BETTER LIFE

Realistic and optimistic are the two great qualities to have together.

The combination leads you to the success.

When you want to succeed at something, think about WHY you do it(purpose), WHAT you do, and HOW you do it.

Remember; Rome was not built in a day.

every effort you make makes a tremendous one.

Don't hold on to the result.

Appreciate what you do now, which means seeing the process.

So, you are happy forever.

The Key word is the now.

What can you do now? What do you want now? What do you want to make out of the now?

Don't limit yourself don't draw a line
Never compromise you

How?

> Try new things
> Focus on the one you like

Whenever you have a difficulty,

You should choose to be happy.

You should stand tall.

Love yourself, be proud of yourself.

All the ego is in your head.

Nothing else matters but your achievement.

What you should focus on

1. The now
2. The short-term goals and long-term goals.

<u>Do you want to die or live?</u>

<u>Do you want to negative or happy?</u>

People change.

People change **every day.**

When the sun rises, there is another self.

Time passes by second by second.

I feel life is going slow but fast.

This present moment has the most power.

The biggest advice I can tell is

Enjoy the now!!

Everything is about perspectives.

Everything is about the balance.

Anyone body can be the happiest person in the world by having **11** steps.

1. Be conscious of who you are while accepting your weaknesses.
2. Appreciate each moment, each day
3. Always seek inspiration
4. Focus on what you are passionate about
5. Keep reminding yourself of what means important to you
6. Love yourself
7. Have a goal
8. Control your emotions
9. Enjoy living in this world
10. Practicing zen
11. Predict your future.

Printed in the United States
by Baker & Taylor Publisher Services